The I Wills According to SAINT JAMES: Book Two

By Synthia SAINT JAMES

ISBN-13: 978-0615987620
ISBN-10: 0615987621

DEDICATION

This book is dedicated to my beautiful and amazing mother Hattie. Thank you for the treasure that you are, and for all the gifts of love and wisdom that you share.

I will renew my spirit with the changing of each season.

I will choose my words wisely because words have life.

I will love freely and accept my vulnerability.

I will use my inner resources of power for positive change.

I will share my loving touch through words of encouragement.

I will recapture the time that I feel I have lost.

I will give myself permission to be happy.

I will keep a positive attitude to ward off needless worry.

I will nourish and maintain the current that keeps me connected to the Creator.

I will make the time to breathe in all the beautiful colors of the universe.

I will cultivate the development of my spirit.

I will value the gift of true friendship.

I will create my life as I would create a work of art.

I will control my emotions for the good.

I will forgive so that I may be forgiven in return.

I will work with what I know.

I will spend more time listening rather than speaking.

I will nurture my sense of humor.

I will allow for my desires to flow freely.

I will take action only when my mind is clear.

I will cultivate my powers of endurance.

I will learn to freely adapt to life's many changes.

I will give my mind all the needed time to listen, absorb and accept.

I will celebrate the diversity of humankind.

I will remain keenly aware of outside influences and choose wisely.

I will protect my inner spirit from intrusion.

I will learn to relax and enjoy.

I will make good use of kind and gentle words.

I will lift others up with my joys.

I will empower myself and others through the words that I speak.

I will accept and process all of my feelings and intuitions.

I will create my own perfect times.

I will keep my mind, body and spirit highly tuned.

I will always hold dear my mother's love.

I will practice self-determination.

I will be persistent.

I will be responsible for my human rights.

I will blend with the harmony of nature.

I will allow myself to continue to learn and grow.

I will make time for the new.

I will hold close to my heart all my precious memories.

I will change for the better all the things that I can change.

I will breathe out all that is negative and breathe in refreshing positivity.

I will create new thoughts and experience new things.

I will search my soul for the answers.

I will make the most of every single second, moment, hour and day.

I will be aware of all that crosses my path.

I will celebrate each season of my life's cycle.

I will make a residential space in my heart for peace.

I will feel and share my compassion with others.

I will practice the law of nonresistance.

I will dwell in my freedom.

I will maintain a common sense attitude.

I will be grateful for all of life's blessings.

I will direct my inner thoughts to still waters.

I will create a good life for myself.

I will indulge in the music that uplifts my soul.

I will be still, listen, and believe.

I will live my life to the very fullest.

I will accept that my life is mine to enjoy.

I will ease my sadness with the memories of my many joys.

I will center myself and find my right answers in my heart.

I will dance, dance and dance whenever the spirit hits me.

I will give thanks every single day for the blessings that life has given me.

I will share my blessings with others.

I will use my powers to edge out all negativity from my life's path.

I will choose to be who I am.

I will dwell in a place of knowledge and then share my gifts.

I will set my mind and spirit courses high and continue to soar.

I will happily embrace all that is new and good.

I will use my inner spirit resources of energy to heal.

I will keep the eyes of my mind and spirit wide open and alert.

I will create new and better habits to replace those in need of replacement.

I will stay in tuned to my inner voice and spirit.

I will work in preparation for the gifts of happiness.

I will insist on my private times to re-center and re-set my rhythms.

I will find many sources of joy during my life's journey.

I will cultivate all my enthusiasms.

I will learn to become calm and peaceful in response to negativities.

I will paint and create only positive life pictures.

I will thrive on my self-confidence.

I will pray for spiritual enlightenment daily.

I will envision myself always in the best of my desired circumstances.

I will look for the good in all.

I will choose my words with love.

I will recognize my true needs and desires.

I will cultivate the power of acceptance.

I will share my true feelings.

I will follow my visions to unforeseen places.

I will slow my pace down as needed.

I will take the time to notice and appreciate all the beauty surrounding me.

I will cultivate the power of patience.

I will remain true to myself first.

I will develop a keen level of common sense.

I will transform from the inside out when needed.

I will feel free to ask for the things that I need.

I will only speak truths.

I will seek and find all that I desire in my life.

I will make the time to let my mind drift.

I will experience all the amazing things that my life has to offer.

www.ingramcontent.com/pod-product-compliance
Lightning Source LLC
LaVergne TN
LVHW020650100826
845148LV00012B/2412

* 9 7 8 0 6 1 5 9 8 7 6 2 0 *